ONE DIRECTION

Anne M. Raso

Andrews McMeel
Publishing, LLC

Kansas City • Sydney • London

Produced by

DOWNTOWN
BOOKWORKS INC.

President
Julie Merberg
Senior Vice President
Patty Brown
Editorial Assistant
Sara DiSalvo
Editorial Intern
Emily Simon
Designer
Brian Michael Thomas/
Our Hero Productions
Special Thanks
Sarah Parvis, Sunny Blue,
Caroline Bronston, and
Melanie Rosenberg

**Andrews McMeel
Publishing, LLC**
an Andrews McMeel
Universal company
1130 Walnut Street, Kansas
City, Missouri 64106
www.andrewsmcmeel.com

13 14 15 16 TEP 10 9 8 7 6
5 4 3

Library of Congress Control
Number: 2012911290

ISBN: 978-1-4494-2953-9

CONTENTS

ONE DIRECTION MANIA

The year 2012 was the time . . . the time for a boy band revival . . . the time for the U.K.'s hottest new import: One Direction!

In 2010 the 1D guys—Harry Styles, Niall Horan, Liam Payne, Zayn Malik, and Louis Tomlinson—wowed *The X Factor's* U.K. audience, but 2012 made them a worldwide phenomenon. 1D headed for America in January 2012 and they've been keeping U.S. audiences "up all night" ever since.

It seems like a lifetime ago when the guys auditioned as solo artists in 2010 for *The X Factor.* A lot has happened since then, but it all began when *The X Factor* judge and music biz legend Simon Cowell switched things up and made them a group. Simon said he felt a vibe that they should be a band the first time they all stood together on *The X Factor* stage. He was right!

Though One Direction finished third on the seventh season of *The X Factor,* a frenzied fan fever broke out all across the U.K. Simon signed them to his U.K. company, Syco Records, and within a year they had signed another big-cash contract with Sony Records in the U.S.

The boys really knew they had blown up with the U.S. pop crowd when they

arrived in L.A. in January 2012 to tape a guest appearance on the popular Nickelodeon show *iCarly*. Hundreds of girls were waiting for them at the airport gate. The guys were amazed, and their meteoric rise to fame proved the power of Twitter, YouTube, Facebook, and Tumblr.

By the time March rolled around, those hundreds of fans had multiplied into millions. The guys had a hit single—"What Makes You Beautiful"—and were opening for the Big Time Rush tour. *Up All Night* made them the first British boy band to debut in the U.S. at #1. The guys were in the Big Apple at the time, performing two Radio City Music Hall shows with BTR,

LIAM:

"We are ourselves. People enjoy what we do because we don't hide anything." **(Today)**

HARRY:

"I can't imagine not being with them [the other 1D guys] every day. We're very lucky."
(www.welovepopmag.co.uk)

attending the "orange carpet" premiere of the *Big Time Movie,* and doing all sorts of radio, TV, and in-store appearances. A U.S. headlining tour was announced and soon enough international tour dates were added to take them all the way through September 2013! In May of 2012, *Up All Night* was certified double platinum—over two million albums sold!

There's more—in May the boys headed to Stockholm to start working on their next CD due to drop in late 2012. They released a live DVD called *Up All Night: The Live Tour* on May 29, and in June they announced they would start working on a

3-D documentary movie due out in 2013. Fans can't wait to see what's next, but 1D is about something deeper than fame—friendship. Said Zayn in *One Direction Invades the USA* tribute magazine, "Since we got together, we [each] made four best friends. For us, that's the most amazing part."

He added with a smile in the same interview, "We're just going to keep doing what we're doing and see what happens."

→ ZAYN:

"Before we got together as a band we were kind of each other's competition . . . but as soon as we got put together we all got on really well. We all went to Harry's place and stayed there together to get to know each other." *(Teen Vogue)*

HEAVENLY HARRY

HARRY HAS 'EM LAUGHING!

Harry is happy that so many people feel at ease around him and that the guys rely on him to say something funny to break up a serious silence. Harry is quick to point out that he likes a girl he can yuk it up with. He told *J-14*, "I like real girls—girls who aren't fake. Girls who are just themselves and have a sense of humor."

"I think if you like someone, then you like that person—you shouldn't play games. You should ask them out." (*Tiger Beat*)

HARRY'S BFF

Louis's mom, Johanna, says that when the band was on 2011 Christmas break, Harry asked Louis to spend time with "the fam." Mrs. T says that she liked Harry from the first time she met him. Harry said in a *Vevo Lift* interview, "Since we started at *The X Factor* house, me and Louis always said we would live with each other. That was pretty much what happened." The two were roommates in the Enfield area of North London until just recently when they both bought their own homes.

"I guess I was always one of those 'you only live once' kind of blokes and life is short; you can never know what's going to happen tomorrow." **(Celebrity Bucket List on Tumblr)**

LOVING LIFE'S SIMPLE PLEASURES

Harry's all about being driven and continuing to keep 1D on top, but along the way, he finds the time to calm down from the 1D mania—simple things like catching a movie on a plane, watching TV before bed or after a show, or going to the gym early in the morning. At home, Harry likes to cook healthy veggie stir-fry dishes and other culinary concoctions, especially tacos!

". . . We keep each other grounded. We've got a great team around us helping us with that. We don't take ourselves too seriously, which I think is a big part of it as well. We know this is an amazing opportunity and we're just having fun with it, enjoying ourselves." *(Life Story)*

NOBLE NIALL

WILL NIALL BE DEMI LOVATO'S NEXT BF?

It's interesting that both Demi and Niall have admitted crushes on each other—her admission came during an April 4 chat on MSN UK and his in a video interview on usweekly.com on June 7. Harry added in an usweekly.com YouTube video that Niall would go for Demi "100 percent," and according to Hollywoodlife.com, Demi said to a fan that Niall was "adorable."

"... I still get nervous around girls I like!"
(Tiger Beat)

"My dad and I waxed our legs for charity. It was very painful. Never again. Hahaha!" (*Heat*)

NIALL'S WEIRDEST FAN GIFT

Niall has been handed lots of fun gifts by fans, but Louis revealed that Niall was sent an actual lamb! The lamb's whereabouts are unknown right now, but we're sure that Niall would have either given it to a farm or a friend who loves unusual pets.

"I like someone who can take a bit of banter!" (*Teen Now*)

HIS FAVORITE FEATURE

Niall is modest about his sweet-faced blond looks. *We Love Pop* asked him what his favorite body part was, and he said, "My eyes. It's the only thing I do like about my body. I feel awkward talking about it actually."

"I'm still in shock about how quickly everything has happened. When we go on a radio show or we get asked for autographs, we still have to pinch ourselves." (*Life Story*)

LOVELY LOUIS

LOUIS: LOYAL BRIT

Louis is proud to be from Doncaster, South Yorkshire, England, and can still be seen playing football on the local field on a rare off day. With 1D's success, he's really the big man about town now—and it hasn't gone to his head. He has told journalists that he wouldn't want to have been raised anywhere else!

"Live life for the moment because everything else is uncertain!" **(Twitter)**

LOUIS'S BETCHA-DIDN'T-KNOW FACTS

⇨ He was born with the last name Austin, but later took his stepdad's last name!

⇨ Says the best Christmas present he ever received was a new mattress from his mom.

⇨ Louis was in a high school band called the Rogues. Their playlist included "Hey There Delilah" by the Plain White T's, and "I'm a Believer" by the Monkees.

⇨ Louis loves his purple chinos. "They sound disgusting, but they look cool," he told *Now*.

"I'd like to adopt a chimpanzee and build an eternal friendship. That would be amazing."
(*On Air With Ryan Seacrest*)

LOUIS'S BOY BAND IDOL

All the 1D guys have musical influences, but for Louis it's Robbie Williams, who first came to popularity with Take That in the '90s. He told *Now,* "I've always loved Robbie. He's just so cheeky, he can get away with anything. His performances are unbelievable. We met a lot of celebrities on *The X Factor* and he was one of the nicest."

"As long as we've got somewhere to sleep, a bowl of cereal, and a coloring book we'll be fine." **(Nokia)**

ZANY ZAYN

HIS "OUTSIDER" DAYS TURNED HIM INTO AN ADVENTURER

Zayn, an East Bowling, U.K., native, says that he felt out of place in school due to his mixed heritage. Zayn changed schools three times and the third, Tong High School, was the charm. He's never been afraid to try new places and opportunities—and he says that he really tried out for *The X Factor* just for the experience!

"My style is more urban than the rest of the group." **(Hot 96.7)**

ZAYN: GEEK AT HEART

Zayn doesn't care that people think some of his interests and likes are geeky. He readily admits to:

- ⇨ Loving Harry Potter books and movies
- ⇨ Liking scary movies that others think are cheesy
- ⇨ Drawing cartoons
- ⇨ Collecting comic books

"I am a big believer in work hard, play hard!"
(*Tatler*)

"I'm the shy one of the group." **(Hot 96.7)**

ZAYN: HE LOVES SIMON COWELL

Zayn has described Simon Cowell as just one of the boys and, like the other lads, calls him "Uncle Simon." Of course, Simon is and always will be the final word when it comes to 1D. So it's no wonder he hasn't okayed Zayn's latest idea of 1D being a "judge" for *The X Factor!* "I'm sure [five 1D boys in one chair] would be very interesting to watch actually," Zayn told entertainment.stv.tv.

LOVEABLE LIAM

LIAM: THE OLD-FASHIONED KIND

Liam is a lover of old-time music, particularly Bing Crosby. He's admitted that if he didn't make it as a singer, he would be in business with his dad, Geoff, building airplanes, or he would be a fireman! He'd make a great firefighter—he likes doing weight training to stay in shape.

"It's strange going from being totally unknown to being on the front of magazines." *(J-14)*

"I'm the cleanest of all the boys; Louis is the messiest!" (*Tiger Beat*)

LIAM: GOING WAY BACK

Liam first sang in public at age five, but did you know that Liam first entered *The X Factor* competition in 2008? Yep! Out of 182,000 contestants entered, he made the top 24 for boys under 25. That must have been nerve-racking!

"I think the whole thing, boy band, it's a little bit of a dirty word. They say it's not a good thing to be in a boy band. We want to change that. We want to make the boy band cool. It's not just about dancing and dressing the same." (*HitFix.com*)

LIAM KEEPS THE OTHER BOYS ON TRACK

⇨ Liam is the first guy to speak up if there is a problem with the other guys (not that there are a lot of them) and he makes useful suggestions

⇨ Liam's always there with a shoulder to cry on

⇨ He keeps the other guys' pranks from going too far

⇨ The other guys say that he needs to let his hair down a bit

"I was a bit of a naughty boy at school. I was often called into the headmistress's office . . . I used to have water fights in the toilets and climb on the roof to get footballs back." **(The Sun)**

STAX OF FACTS

The 411 on the Fabulous Five—some we bet you never knew!

HARRY'S 411

- ➯ Was born on February 1, 1994.

- ➯ Fave chain restaurant is T.G.I. Friday's.

- ➯ Can speak French.

- ➯ Had his first kiss when he was eleven.

- ➯ His hidden talents are knitting and juggling.

- ➯ Does not like mayonnaise.

- ➯ According to unrealitytv.com, Harry is being considered to play rock star Mick Jagger in an upcoming film.

LIAM'S 411

- Was born on August 29, 1993.

- Considered the "daddy" of the group.

- Says that he scrunches himself up in the covers at night.

- Says that great childhood memories include going to Disneyland and winning a swimming race.

- The grooming product he can't live without is hair wax.

- Claims to be teaching Zayn how to improve his dancing.

- Has turtles named Boris and Archimedes.

LOUIS'S 411

⇨ Was born on Christmas Eve in 1991.

⇨ Is the oldest member of One Direction.

⇨ Does not like tattoos.

⇨ Has four sisters.

⇨ Loves French ice cream.

⇨ Loves the music of both Elvis and the Beatles.

⇨ Was a huge Pokémon fan when he was younger.

ZAYN'S 411

- ⇨ Was born on January 12, 1993.

- ⇨ First name means "beautiful" in Arabic.

- ⇨ Despite being in a boy band, he admits that he doesn't like dancing onstage.

- ⇨ Suffers from a fear of heights (acrophobia) and is also scared of the dark.

- ⇨ His left ear is pierced.

- ⇨ His father is from Pakistan.

- ⇨ His favorite hobby is drawing.

NIALL'S 411

- ⇨ Was born on September 13, 1993.

- ⇨ Favorite book is *To Kill a Mockingbird*.

- ⇨ Claims to be afraid of birds, especially when they fly into a house.

- ⇨ Screamed when he met Justin Bieber—but walked out of the room to do so!

- ⇨ Favorite chain restaurant is Nando's (he loves their famous Portuguese-style Peri-Peri chicken)—American 1D fans can check out Nando's locations in Washington, D.C., and Silver Spring, Maryland.

5 FAVES OF 5 FAVES!

All the 1D dish that you wish!

FAVE MOVIE

Harry: *Love Actually*
Liam: All the *Toy Story* movies
Louis: *Forrest Gump*
Zayn: *Grease*
Niall: *Taken* or *Grease* (can't decide)

NICKNAMES

Harry: Harold, Barry, and Hazza
Liam: Daddy Direction and Daddy Liam
Louis: Hughy, Lou, Tommo, and Boo Bear
Zayn: Wayn, Z, and DJ Malik
Niall: Kyle, Nialler, and Ni

ZAYN:

"Us five being put together is the best thing that's happened to all of us." (*Life Story*)

FAVE SONG

Harry: "Shine on You Crazy Diamond" by Pink Floyd

Liam: "Happy Birthday" (because it gets him presents)

Louis: "Look After You" by the Fray

Zayn: "Thriller" by Michael Jackson

Niall: "Viva La Vida" by Coldplay

CELEB CRUSH

Harry: Confessed to MTV that he would like to date Kate Winslet, Angelina Jolie, or Kate Moss

Liam: Gorgeous U.K. songbird Leona Lewis

Louis: The former *X Factor* judge, singer, and U.K. fashion icon Cheryl Cole (although his first crush at age six was Emma Watson)

Zayn: Katy Perry

Niall: Demi Lovato

FAVE FOOD

Harry: Tacos

Liam: Chocolate

Louis: Pizza and pasta

Zayn: Chicken and samosas

Niall: Pizza and Nando's chicken

HEART SMART

The 1D crew talks about love and romance!

HARRY: ◄

"I don't have a type, because with some girls, I might not find them attractive immediately but then I do like them because their personality is so attractive. I like someone who could get on with my parents; it's important that my family like her, too."
(onedirectionweekly.com)

ZAYN: ◄

"You need to take risks to find love . . . obviously having to split up with people is difficult . . . I do get quite emotional actually. I'm a bit of a softy. I tend to keep it to myself if I'm feeling upset about something, though. I'll put my headphones on and block it out."
(We Love Pop)

→ NIALL:

"I'm an emotional guy, so I don't have to worry about a girl trying to get me to open up." **(Irish Daily Mirror)**

→ LOUIS:

"I'm a bit old-fashioned and I like the idea of going to the cinema and then an Italian restaurant . . . I'm a bit of a joker. I can be a romantic, but not too sickly—I like to keep it on a level . . . You have to get the banter in there, too, otherwise you scare the girl away." **(Now)**

→ LIAM:

Currently "taken," Liam seeks out "someone who's cheeky but quiet, too. A bit shy as well—I don't like really loud girls." **(Us)**

1D: GOING IN CRAZY DIRECTIONS

Pranks, fan stories, and just plain tattling on each other!

⇨ **Harry**'s famous for being a prankster, so it isn't surprising his band mates retaliated on his eighteenth birthday. Harry was chilling at a hotel when the lads doused him with four ice-cold buckets of water! Really chilling!

⇨ Ever since **Louis** claimed carrots as one of his favorite foods, girls have held up signs at shows saying, "Louis, I love carrots!" A few have even dressed up in carrot costumes! And so did Louis during the 2011 tour of *The X Factor*!

⇨ **Liam** told *Us Weekly* that he does have his quirks, including a totally unique one. He revealed, "I have a strange fear of spoons . . . I eat cereal in two cups—one with milk and one with cereal!"

⇨ All the guys are expert prank callers, but **Harry** and **Louis** seem to be the kings of this "sport"! Harry's good at American accents, but Louis's English "lady voice" is just too high and wacky to be believable.

⇨ **Zayn** had a fan experience he'll never forget. "This girl touched my hand and then fainted," he told *USA TODAY*. "That was probably the weirdest thing I ever experienced. I've seen girls fainting in crowds and stuff, like when we were performing, but I'd never seen anything like it that close. She just completely fainted, like, passed out on the floor."

⇨ The whole group admits to being tweetaholics, but **Louis** says that he is the one who is following the most 1D fans!

1D FAQS

Answers to the questions that Directioners ask most!

Q: How long did it take *Up All Night* to reach gold status in the U.S.?

A: One month—and it sold 176,00 copies the first week it was out! By May 2012, it had gone double platinum!

Q: Liam is open about having a girlfriend in interviews and her name is Danielle Peazer. How long have they been together?

A: Danielle is a dancer and he met her when she was dancing on *The X Factor*. They have been dating since December 2010 and the rest of the guys love her. Said Liam to *Us Weekly,* "The boys get on really well with her. They're all good mates."

Q: How can a fan meet the band?

A: Liam explained that the boys are still doing meet and greets via contests that give winners wristbands to get into special events. Keep an eye on their official Web sites and listen to your local radio stations for contests when the guys are coming to your area. There are also VIP ticket packages that include meet and greets in most towns.

Q: Are there any other 1D projects besides the second album and the ongoing *Up All Night* Tour?

A: While the guys say that the talk of a Nick show back in spring was nothing more than talk, they do have a 3-D feature film planned for 2013. It will be about the group's real-life antics on and offstage.

Q: What is the name of the upcoming 1D album?

A: As of summer 2012, the album has no name, but the band is saying that it has a lot more "live" and "raw" feel, including a lot more guitar work. They recorded in four towns including Stockholm and L.A., and this explains the big gap in summer tour dates from July to December.

1D'S SWEET TWEETS

The best way to follow what the guys are doing at the immediate moment is to follow them on Twitter . . . and their tweets are mighty sweet!

Harry (@Harry_Styles)

I feel like I've woken up with suddenly more facial hair and a deeper voice. Thank you for all your lovely birthday messages.

Dropping your sunglasses down the toilet is a mistake you would think that you'd learn from. Apparently not.

Liam (@Real_Liam_Payne)

Excited I'm gonna get to following over 5000 of you lovely people today :)

I'm so excited to travel the world and do gigs all over next year its gonna be amazing

Zayn (@zaynmalik)

In life we give and we take, let me tell you now you will never get as much as you give.

This bath is amazing :) thumbs up aha

Niall (@NiallOfficial)

The buzz u get off the audience, like today im sick, but the audience pushed me through

Wow just noticed! 4 million followers, you guys are amazing! Thank you soo much, love all you

Louis (@Louis_Tomlinson)

Massive thank you to everyone who has ever supported us. We would be nowhere without you and I assure you we never take it for granted :) xx

So I stand at a new crossroad in my life . . . Do I order another bowl of Corn Pops or not?

1D DISCOGRAPHY

Up All Night (Released March 13, 2012, after being rolled back from March 20, 2012, due to popular demand)

TRACK LISTING

1. "What Makes You Beautiful"
2. "Gotta Be You" (2012 U.S. version)
3. "One Thing"
4. "More Than This"
5. "Up All Night"
6. "I Wish"
7. "Tell Me a Lie"
8. "Taken"
9. "I Want"
10. "Everything About You"
11. "Same Mistakes"
12. "Save You Tonight"
13. "Stole My Heart"

THE VIDEOS (All from the *Up All Night* album, all released in first half of 2012)
"What Makes You Beautiful"
"Gotta Be You"
"One Thing"

HOME VIDEO *Up All Night: The Live Tour DVD* (released March 29, 2012)

THE 2013 TOUR
The guys start the tour ball rolling for what will certainly be "Lucky 2013" on February 22, where they headline for three nights at the O2 Arena in London. This set of shows is being heralded as their biggest and flashiest yet.

Then right afterward, they are going to Glasgow, Scotland's huge Scottish Exhibition and Conference Centre! They will continue to wow in Scotland, Ireland, and the U.K. though April, and then the U.S. gets them back in June! Though exhausting to think about, these shows will be a truly "beautiful" experience for 1D fans.

1D WEB SITES MANIA

The boys blew up in the U.S. before they even had a record out thanks to social media—and there are more sites devoted to the lads every day. Here are the best!

OFFICIAL SITE

Onedirectionmusic.com
   keeps fans up to date on all appearances, 1D tweets, merchandise, media coverage, and more

RECOMMENDED FAN SITES

Onedirectionfans.org
   cute pics and updates from the most dedicated Directioners

Onedirectionsource.com
   this English site is "all that and a spot of tea"

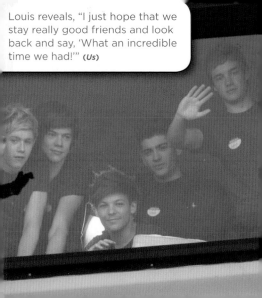

Louis reveals, "I just hope that we stay really good friends and look back and say, 'What an incredible time we had!'" *(Us)*

PHOTO CREDITS